The Other Italy

David Clive Price

The Olive Press

No ordinary travel book, this personal view of the lingering continuity of traditional life in the countryside, provinces and ancient towns of Italy takes the reader on a journey into the past, one steadily disappearing throughout the lands of the Mediterranean.

In a series of close-ups and panoramic scenes, there are meetings with the farmers Livia and Gino, the local choir, Parise the share cropper, the workers at the olive press, citizens and mourners in Crotone, the ghost inhabitants of Matera, and actors and transvestites in Naples. The books ends with the Ruins Management, Pompeii seen as a symbol of this other Italy, challenged by all kinds of natural, ecological and man-made disaster, and yet somehow still surviving.

'Lovely book....a strong undying charm like a scent for the past.' The Literary Review, London.

For Livia and Gino

" Ten minutes from the Autostrada I discovered the other Italy . . . For the first time in my life it upset me to meet men and women in houses which could not really be called houses, to take into account existences which were not sophisticated, lived out by people who had on the other hand a profound human dignity. "

*Testimony of a young volunteer
to the Italian earthquake zone, 1982*

An excerpt from Chapter One was first broadcast on BBC Radio 3 April 15th 1981, under the title 'We Northern Visitors'.

First published in 1983 by The Olive Press
30 Pembroke Road, London, E17
Copyright © 1983 David Clive Price

ISBN: 9781477643082

About the Author

David Clive Price is the author of the novels *Alphabet City* and *Chinese Walls*, and the travel books *The Other Italy*, *Travels in Japan*, *A Korean Journey*, *Secrets of the Forbidden City* and *Buddhism: The Fabric of Life in Asia.* He has also translated into English *The Scent of India* by poet, film director and novelist Pier Paolo Pasolini. After graduating with a doctorate in History from Cambridge University, he spent some years a lecturer in Italy, where he farmed olives and began to write. Subsequently, he travelled widely in the Far East and was speechwriter for the HSBC Group for the handover of Hong Kong to China. He has written extensively on the cultures, people and traditions of many countries throughout the world. He divides his time between London, Italy and the Philippines.

Contents

Part 1: Close-Up

1. My Country Town
2. The Choir Practices
3. Paris
4. The Olive Press

Part 2: Panorama

5. The 'Stones' of Matera
6. A Funeral in Crotone
7. In the Search of Verga
8. A Neapolitan Sceneggiata

Epilogue: The Ruins Management

Author's Books

Part I: Close Up

1. My Country Town

Two or three times a week I walk up into town on what was once the salt-mule track to Florence, in order to shop. It is a chore, especially if it's raining, but there is always some little surprise to boost the day. A view clear over to the snow-capped Apennines, the sea just glinting along the Pisan coast, local farmers cutting olives or mending a wall. A funeral attended by black-hooded monks and a file of mourners on its way to the cemetery, its electric candles all lit up at night. The market on Saturdays. A snake of traffic through the streets or the carpet silence even on Summer nights. And then the food. Not only the shops for coffee and tea in bulk or the well stocked family grocers but also the pastry shops with almond cakes, the little greengrocer with artichokes and salad and tomatoes. My favourite grocer is a diminutive Edith Piaf lady, who courts the best society and gives me a *panettone* or bottle of *spumante* each Christmas. But many of the shopkeepers are characters. The egg lady, small, fat and round, with the cheeks of a country girl, is a rabid anti-clericalist and supporter of the red flag. She and the chicken man always ask me what I am growing. So do the banker teller, Edith Piaf, and the sly seller of plants under the Piazza arch. It is a small, proud town, with an intimacy – and often a slowness – which requires my patience. Now I stand almost casually in the butchers as the women push in front, not so much pushing as moving from A to B, from need to realisation, quite instinctively, as the slit carcass of a cow hangs there dripping from its chains. A smell of fresh lamb, of dark coffee in plastic bags as I make my way down the steep hill path, where I often meet Livia.

Livia is responsible for my coming to the valley, for turning me into a smallholder. It is through her and Gino that I have come to know something of the other Italy.

She is a hardy, rather stumpy woman of uncertain youth (she is actually 70) who has lived in this valley all her life and 15 years ago moved into the school-mistress' large farmhouse as its tenant and as a kind of housekeeper to the English or French families who came like me to rent the house in the valley. She has brought up two strapping sons and a daughter, has now six grand-children who live close by, has created with Gino two farms, rises at five in the morning to get their son Mario off to work, has a heart condition, works to earn extra money on the villas of some holidaying Milanese, is hostess to the English visitors, and cooks or cleans regularly for 'her men'. Yet she is still unable to consider biting any hands which feed her, doesn't blame the *padroni* at all and only complains about the fact that she gets older but the work remains the same. She knew that the European elections were a very minor charade in comparison to the way the whole telephone system was blocked so that she couldn't get through to her son, on military service in Padua. Not a woman to take advantage of . . . yet such a generosity of spirit. She has *enjoyed* her life, her English visitors, their children she had to nurse. Livia will carry your bags on her head, give you mountains of produce, fill your wine glass to the brim (taking nothing for herself), make a fire for your arrival, produce linen and towels, bring a message at dead of night and ask nothing in return.

Gino, her husband, is older and leaner – like a stick in fact – but with hollowed-out, smiling eyes that are fascinating in themselves. He has a splutter of a laugh, a lively sense of irony and a way with proverbs which makes nonsense of received knowledge; received from the television that is. Yet he does watch TV, tired as he is at night. It gives a bit of company, he explains – company provided by country neighbours and little festivals in the days when there weren't so many cars and 'weekends' and tours and discos. Indeed the strongest local voice, the most powerful forum of all, *is* nowadays the television. Some local restaurants will have it on even during serving hours. It stands in a dominant position over the tables like some myopic brother. There are two retailers of televisions in the town, with the result that almost no farmhouse, even the remotest and wildest, has remained without an aerial. The children of old *contadini* make sure that the set is also a colour one, preferably with big screen, and Gino and Livia would have it on loudly while I was eating there; that is, until they realised I didn't demand it of them. Most citizens of the town watch television after a small evening meal and drinking a glass of wine. Yet I often wonder what Gino thinks as Livia cooks and he is told to eat German sausages (they make their own), to drink beer with his meal as the only way to digest properly, to wear American jeans.

How can I describe the way that Gino watches television? A dog hearing a high noise perhaps, who knows very well that when it stops he'll go off to find a bone. He breaks away from the high-kicking dance girls – his favourite – to check the animals, pour some wine from the demi-john, water the tomatoes. Football and politics make him sleep, right there to the kitchen table, cap pushed back on his head. Gino has never been to Florence. In fact he is regarded as something of a fool by his own family, who scorn him when he says anything about the world outside. He doesn't know where Austria is or England or about money rates or even about new cars. He only knows how to make walls or new vines and speak his strong dialect. Without him, however, I would never have succeeded to buy a farmhouse and to make it work, without his fox wisdom or Livia's clear head. They taught me how to farm too, gently, without too many reproofs.

I visit them less now, perhaps only once a month, although their house is only ten minutes down the hill. So if I go it's a special occasion, perhaps a meal together.

A winter evening in recent years for example. Only a little snow but the night is silent, with the fountain drip-dripping out the back. Dinner with Livia and Gino, plus Mario for a change. He has a shot a wild boar and duck while out on the hunt with his friends. Livia provides the *fegatelli* (little bags of chopped liver) along with minestrone soup of her own vegetables. The meal is simple and good. My hosts yawn honestly towards 9:30 p.m. (they rise at 5 a.m.), still being indulgent to loud complaining 20-year old Mario (the sauce was not good enough, the duck was not tender) as the huge moon looms over the hills and conversation touches on farm-workers without insurance, the abandoned agricultural sector of Italian society, officialdom, locals, taxes. I feel myself back in some antique, Biblical world.

And then the stoicism of this couple. Livia with heart trouble, especially when the wind blows strongly, standing at the arched cellar door of *Mulinetto* after carrying wood to us on her head, that kerchiefed head leaning on her propped fist, crooked legs in boots to match the symmetry. Biblical again. Gino's long spare figure operated on recently, now silhouetted scything the last square of grass down the hill.

Sunday evening means *Ballo Liscio*, classical folk dance, in the hall of the local bar. Little or no sign of drunkenness. A squat single man in his fifties, with ripe paunch, explains to me the technique of presenting the body elegantly to your partner, of cutting *una bella figura*. A live band playing mountain polkas as the couples swirl, children and youths too., with vivacity but great technique. Waltzes: a generic term. No-one carries a drink into the dance hall. One or two will offer wine to the foreigners, but usually a coffee and quick brandy for real drinkers. Otherwise with women and children around, there is no wild carousing. Watching and not watching each other. A dramatic movement is unusual here and I have never seen a fight.

Politeness is much more evident. Here it takes form if *Buon Giorno* or *Buona Sera*, but also of titles, Almost anyone who has gone through school will be called *Dottore*, and an older version will automatically become *Professore, Ingegnere, Maresciallo, Capo*; the list is endless (and mainly male). Sometimes Livia injects more *Professore* into her speech than she has things to say. The titles are relics of an old, crumbling respect system and clear social division – like entrances into houses. If an Englishman's social home is a castle, so it is for a local from here, who will not set foot into another's cellar without a preliminary *permesso* and a permission-giving *s'accomodi* or *prego*. An entrance into a house is a ritual. Livia's slippers left by the front door remind me of some Brahmin or Japanese rite, even though she is changing, quite practically, into boots. A glass of something may be offered if you are not expected to a meal, probably vermouth rather than the more ordinary wine, but you are not expected to stay too long if there is work to be done. You will never be asked to leave. Yet, when actually outside of your front door, your land – you – are a highway, common property. There is no fenced land here. Normal human curiosity and a kind of animal rubbing-together will combine to make any privacy laughable – a nook for writing, or eating lunch, or reading the paper outside a shop. It is simply taken for granted that people don't hide away from each other but generally perform in public, showing a certain discipline but also formalising indiscretion. In this way various necessary things are imparted to others. Certain families who come to get water at the communal fountain make friendly comments on the progress of my work and prospects. Indiscretion is made discreet, like children. The bars in town repeat the pattern. No confrontation, but a formalised and observant doing-of-nothing. The papers are read and some daily news discussed. Men are served, sometimes by women behind the bar, and the bar-owners are mainly Sicilian or Sardegnan. Sometimes the bars are crowded, particularly on Saturday morning, but very little is actually consumed. A coffee. A glass of wine. A roll. Men are always playing cards in the back rooms; those back rooms – a shabby light, a billiard table perhaps, smoke filing, hats back on heads and the murmur of card placings, a face with eyebrows arched watching your progress to the toilet (amusement, contempt?), a joke on someone's name or what he has said, endless ritual.

And despite their apparently secondary status women also have their own voice here. They are the shoppers, the food preparers, often the shopkeepers themselves, but this allows them their own forums. They group in Edith Piaf's shop on a Monday morning or stand around the (female) butcher's, often commenting with amusement on general male inadequacies. They gossip in the restaurant kitchens. They are the regular cemetery visitors, the flower sellers, the office workers and family peeresses. They are a race apart, the child-bearers, but also legitimate objects of male fancy in the streets. Any female can expect staring, especially if foreign. And to judge from night cars on the country paths and the receptacles left there, this results in some clandestine activity. Nowadays.

People say that promiscuity shows the weakening hold of the Church on conscience, permissiveness strengthened through TV's powerful influence, becoming part of the new bourgeois Italy. Perhaps there is some truth in this. Although Catholicism is a natural part of daily life here, the Church itself is the object of a curious reticence, almost amounting to indifference, especially among the country people. As if their independence came first, a stern moral uprightness second, and clericalism a poor third. Everyone brings flowers to the cemetery and takes part in saints' days and family communions, but actual church-going, or any active sign of evangelism at work is strangely faint-hearted. As if priests were to be taken with a pinch of salt, like doctors and their prescriptions.

Indeed, despite the alienation promoted from outside, the town and its surrounding countryside have their own realities to offer: woodless hills, soft, topped by a line of cypresses, a farm and haystack, a grove of olives with shadows patterning the beige soil, smoke rising from allotments signifying human activity, abandoned convents, the glint of a river snaking towards the hazy crowded coast. Snow, ghostly and silent for a few days in winter, olive trees like giant meringues. Medieval Tuscany again. In spring sometimes squalid low rain for days, the roof tiles drip-dripping and wood pieces fizzling the time away. But a drama. Almost always a drama.

Much of the land is farmed on a large, technically sophisticated scale. There are small factories for wine and olive oil, for salt and marble, for sunflowers and strawberries, but some land is still cultivated on a share-cropping or tenant farmer basis. Few can manage without at least a half-day job in some local industry or town. But the oxen yoked to their plough testify to the survival of an ancient world, individual skills. Binding vines, cutting the olives, chopping bamboo, hand saws and axes – these are aspects of traditional knowledge unsurpassed by often borrowed or half owned tractors. And these skills are still a family patronage. If some are leaving for the cities, the landscape is somehow still peopled.

By men of the hunt too. In September, the season's opening fills the air around here with the noise of early morning warfare, consistent, clumsy, shouts of men at badly-trained dogs, perhaps an injury, and not often much to show. The development of the hunt, with its attendant social kudos and special dress requirements (like a Vietnamese army jacket), its urban devotees, has provoked a natural crisis in the animal kingdom; and in that of the birds particularly. Some locals are asking whether the hunting reserves can remain a part of the landscape, and of the kitchen landscape, without more controls.

Many of our neighbours keep rabbits and chickens. Paris and Leda, a couple who farm the neighbouring land, keep their animals rather cooped up in one hut. Livia keeps hers in hutches. Chickens must be fed, eggs collected, grass of a special sort cut for the rabbits. A chicken is dispatched by a swift wringing of the neck, a rabbit by a bang on the head with a piece of wood. This is all done with an air of discretion, respect for the animal, and complete naturalness. Livia brightly converses as she wrings and plucks a chicken. 'Well, we do eat them, don't we?' she seems to say.

A few donkeys are also to be seen – they were once the main transport, carrying salt to Florence and beyond – but goats are more popular. A goat can be kept on a chain grazing near the house or even far away, keeping the meadows clean. A helpful animal, unlike the quilled porcupines who slyly lumber up to the potato patch at night. And the snakes, which emerge in varying shapes and sizes (only one is really dangerous) in the hot days of June. These, and horses, wild dogs, cuckoos, owls, lizards, toads and tortoises are a constant source of cryptic conversation, amused anecdote and genuine wonder among the inhabitants. Toads and snakes come to visit my fountains, usually grass snakes with green-yellow skins and long elegant movements. Lizards of every size inhabits the walls. A huge owl sometimes sits on the TV aerial. The first cuckoo calls in mid-April. Two weeks later the first swallow arrives in the eave nests. Another two weeks and the fireflies begin to blink out an erratic message in the olive groves. The cat is resident all year, and even during winter hunts and sleeps outside. He sharpens his claws on the wooden pergolas. He also digs in the garden at special moments, but only in the best earth.

The earth is as important to the upper kingdom as to the lower. Most families have some kind of allotment. The climate is relatively mild in winter, the springs are wet, the summers often serene; planting takes a regular course. Naturally there are moments when everyone complains, but in general fresh vegetables are available all year round. Indeed not very much is imported fresh (winter oranges for example) and this puts a special, anticipatory pressure on the nerve labelled *Stomach: what's in store.* The residents of the town are still largely untouched by the deep-freeze culture of the North, where foodstuffs are artificially available the whole year. Much the same applies to meat, especially spring lamb, which is not available in season, and is expensive. But it is also fresh and local.

So the land is intensively, if simply cultivated , the only exceptions being the small but expanding middle class who, rather than a plot of land or a little summer farmhouse, have an obligatory villa at the sea for their holidays and weekends. Yet apparently some sort of planting has a place in everyone's world-view. Here it is a passion which seems to unite all, tenant farmer to bank manager's wife, even if it's only a window box or a few vines - a passion, both aesthetic and practical, connecting the eye to the stomach, the farmer's sculpted terraces to the citizen's purse. And like any great passion, it has its cold centre. The discipline of daily cutting, binding, earth-removing, predicting, feeding, slaughtering, and once more pruning, digging, repairing, feeding, slaughtering. On Market Day a swarm of ladies in black seem to spend their week's savings: in black, dressed in black. On the same day the ladies will carry the lilies and irises they have bought to the cemetery. But life must go on, which means that one must eat - and eat properly.

Livia and Gino cook a chop twice a week, perhaps a wild fowl or chicken on a feast day, but usually home-made pasta or a vegetable soup. They smoke their own ham and sausage, make their own olive oil and wine and tomato preserve, have of course their own vegetables. There is discipline in this abundance, perhaps especially in abundance. There is also a strong sense of being sufficient, of being independent. A personal experience which is at the same time a social one, much as the willed and almost excessive isolation is matched by a distant neighbourliness; the farmer's wife who offers some salad on her way up the track, the 'good evening' and chat with a face one hardly knows at the *Ballo Liscio*. An isolation different to the loneliness of our cities.

Different the sense of time also. Seasons. The sun rising on the golf-course hills to the left, over the house at midday, disappearing west while work continues in the fields until a moon sailing above the opposite farm announces supper. Time governed by clouds, finishing farm work before the rain, shopping curtailed on market day, writing in bed during storms, Monday is often Sunday, or Sunday Friday. A stillness returning amidst activity - and some kind of pact being made. *'Dove si vive, si muore',* a neighbour cheerfully confides to me one day.

I stand stock still for a moment. Suddenly I have the feeling that I have been here before, in some previous life, here in the other Italy. 'Where one lives, one dies'. It is a simple sentence but one which nonetheless seems to express so much of the peasant's stoicism, his view of existence, the eternal and circular process.

2. The Choir Practices

A bitterly cold Monday evening in winter. It is practice night for the local choir, for next week they will travel by coach to Bulgaria on a little concert tour. They are always going to places like Bulgaria, Yugoslavia, Greece, for each September this choir is the host to many others at the 'international festival' in town. At that time the Teatro Persio Flacco, with its severe classical interior and crowded bar, opens its dowdy curtains to several visiting choirs, mainly from Italy, but also from Australia, Switzerland, Greece or Spain. I have been asked to come along tonight by Gianna, a student of archaeology at the University of Siena, so that I may listen to the choir being put through its paces by its priest conductor.

Despite the cold, the choristers file noisily into the arched committee room they have been temporarily leased. It is on the ground floor of a *palazzo* and has iron grilles across the windows. However, the stone walls will make it resonant.

A little embarrassed, I sit and face the forty-strong choir while the Reverendo Maestro, a stout man with glasses and a broad, pale face, searches through his music folders. He glances nervously at me from time to time, and occasionally offers me one of the scores so that I can follow. However, for the liveliest singing there are no scores. The choir knows the songs by heart.

First they warm up with some religious music, a piece by Palestrina. It is dreary stuff, unsuited to their bright nasal voices, but it is obviously intended as training by the conductor. The girls in the front row, fresh-faced and dark with an occasional gibber exception, have to repeat their flowing runs. The basses, many of them with cheeks reddened by stimulus other than the wind, bumble doe-eyed and intolerant through their supporting role, sometime arguing amongst themselves or with the tenors. Those who makes mistakes are easy to spot - the others cringe from them rather obviously or group around the perfectionist of each section. I am relieved when this exercise period is over. I know what this choir can do.

Suddenly we are off. Forty mouths breathe smoke into the frosty air of the room and the glass cabinets shakes as the choir launches into *O Rondinella*, a folk song addressed by an abandoned wife to a travelling minstrel - should he find her love again on his travels through the mountains he must tell him she is waiting. This is followed by a *Ninna-Nanna* typical to the area, a bittersweet lullaby to a new-born baby who brings into the world yet more cares, yet more beauty. The part of the mother is taken by a young girl soloist whose simple expressive voice rises piercingly above the hushed choral accompaniment. Everyone smiles at the end. They enjoyed that. 'Did *you* like it?' asks the priest suspiciously. 'Of course,' I answer truthfully. Whenever it sings like this the choir makes a rich warm sound of such intensity that other choral experiences, indeed daily experiences, fade away. One is there in the mountains, in the life of abandonment, nursing the hope of finding love again, of winning against the *padrone,* or resisting the need to emigrate, of making the earth work, in surroundings provided by the simple beauty of nature. So it is whenever these sharp *uccellini* open their mouths.

It was the same at festival time. Whenever a choir from the plain, from Pisa or Pavia, sang its polite repertoire of refurbished classics or religious music, there was suitable applause from the audience (which included not a few farmers and peasants, sitting up near the front and rocking from side to side enthusiastically). But the real tingle along the spine, the tears in the eyes, came whenever a choir, like the unforgettable one from Sardegna with their folk costume and nasal improvisations, their men standing in a circle to sing, or the mountain choir from Carrara with their paunches and discipline, sang their own songs - the ones they knew as children and which expressed their, and especially their forefathers', struggle for life and love. These choirs are rare - and often ashamed to sing their own tradition. They have to be encouraged to do so. But then, what an awakening!

Each year I hear no more than a tiny handful of these songs, so it is for this reason too that I am at the choir practice. The choir does not disappoint me. After one further gesture to the counter-reformation, they begin to enjoy themselves. One of the favourite types of song is the *contrasto,* a dialogue of some sort between share-cropper and landlord, between Florentine and Senese, between earth and sea, blond and brunette (and lately between America and Russia, or Christian Democrat and Communist). The form is that of an *ottava rima*, a metric form found in both written and oral sources. There is room in the form for improvisation and for satiric, sociological or even political expression. In it the world of the peasant is rarely seen as idyllic. On the contrary, amidst the benefits of their life are seen to coil the twin serpents of exploitation and resignation. *Pasquino and the Padrone,* for example, is a long *contrasto* in twenty octaves, in which the arbitrary division of the farmer's produce is denounced, the arrogance and parasitic nature of the landlords, the elders' resignation which must be countered by the resistance of the younger peasants. Finally Pasquino receives some material assistance from his *padrone,* but only in exchange for allowing his wife to lie with the man. Little wonder that these *contrasti* were sung during the Second World War by the resistance, or in the fields at harvest time (now, sadly, no more). Music, whether concerted in choral form or simply improvised to an accordion, has for centuries been the expression of peasant survival and will. When I hear the rich chords of those repeating choruses, insisting again and again that Ugenia must leave the convent where she has been deposited by her parents and go to live the life of love, or those damning the marshy coats of the Maremma where poverty has forced the labourers to work, or the laments of Venerenda who cannot lie with her boy because neither mother nor father will allow it, it is this peasant strength which seems to speak directly to the heart. It is the same with the *rime* on the massacres of Mussolini, the foolishness and greed of the priest who comes to take a share of the harvest, or the false hopes of emigration.

> *"Sia in America, in Francia o Inghilterra,*
> *il male peggior è lavorar la terra"*

> Whether in America, France or England,
> the worst thing is to work the land.

The choir come to the end of its practice for tonight. The air no longer runs with their breath. Immediately after the last deafening chord they pack up without the slightest sign of regret. Back to business, they seem to say. 'Enjoy it did you?', one or two tenors ask me on the way out.

As soon as I get home I write out my favourite, for I am sure it will not appear at the next festival. There it is all politeness, an announcer (a local journalist with a taste for weak jokes), a prize-giving which awards an Etruscan figurine to each participant, bouquets of flowers and interminable delays to search for a choir which seems to have left for or retreated to the bar. They have no time for this kind of song:

Share Cropper

Good day, landlord sir,
I have come to say goodbye,
The farm gives me no profit,
I am about to let it die.
I work night and day
Just to stay alive.
I give you the keys.
You can make it thrive.

Landlord

O you stupid peasant
and so lacking in shame
You abandon my farm
Because you've made your name.
You have a nice car
and as much as wine as you can down
Now you buy an apartment
close to the town.

Share Cropper

O listen, landlord sir,
I am a ruined man.
If I stay on your farm
I'll be just a sham!
I have a child that goes to school
And now he wants to study.
You claim you have a farm.
Come make your own hands muddy!

Landlord

In nineteen twenty-one
The peasants were a better type
They spoke against the selfish
And their affection was full and ripe
They worked night and day
With strength, as in a dream.
Now you are not happy.
You do it all with a machine!

Share Cropper

In nineteen twenty-one,
For one reason or another
Then you used on them
an ancient cudgel, brother.
If in eighty-two
Twenty-one is now no more
Then the cudgel too
Must be forbidden by the law!

3. Paris

It often seems that Paris came with the house, and indeed the house is now unimaginable without him. He belongs as much as the white cat who lives in his hut, amidst the straw for the rabbits, or the horses which stand in the next field or the swallows who come regularly each year to the house eaves. My first memory of him is that of a man dressed in a blue boiler suit with an armful of bamboo staves, cut very sharp, in one hand and an axe in the other, looking down on me with amusement, interest, and perhaps a slight element of pity as I was shown around the wild lush tangle which constituted the land I took over from the previous owner.

Yet he is not a landowner himself. Paris is a *mezzadro*, his relationship to the land and his absentee *padrone* being the last remnant of that old tradition of Tuscan *mezzadria* which, despite strikes and revolts and agrarian land leagues, reaches back centuries. The geography of Tuscany, with its intensely-cultivated smallholdings and big landlords, was once ideally suited for this system of exploiting - while tolerating - the peasantry. The *poderi,* small and large, were allocated to obedient peasant families who farmed them on a subsistence basis while paying rent to the landlord in the form of land upkeep, a percentage of the crops, a half of the expenses for seed and animal fodder, a half part for any slaughtered animals, the best selection for crops, transport to the granary, to the olive press or to the landlord's agent, a half of the veterinary fees. At the same time the *mezzadro* was forbidden to marry off any of his family without the landlord's permission, to travel or absent himself in any way, to work ground of his own or that of any neighbour (black work) undertake the buying of animals or seasonal work without the agent's permission. In other words, as a result of the 'co-operation' between capital and labour, the *mezzadro* and his family were the moral and physical property of the landlord, and were kept as far as possible from education and from the restless urban proletariat. One might remember this when complaining of the peasant's conservatism.'

Indeed Paris is one if those 'conservative' peasantry, if not in the way commonly intended. For one thing he does not live on the land he cultivates as *mezzadro*. He has an apartment in town, where he has lived for thirty years with his wife Leda. It may now seem that their names are mythological but their jobs are less so. Leda works in a small packing factory, Paris as a transporter of goods , mainly alabaster. His conservatism stems from his extraordinary resilience, his stubbornness. Perhaps he could afford to give up his part of the *podere*, to wave goodbye to his landlord who comes on occasional weekends from Florence. Perhaps he could give up work altogether now that he is approaching the age of a pension. But he will not, because his work is his life, and particularly work on the *podere*. His conversation resides in the sense he has of continuity, of fighting it out on a well-worn path: however easy the nearby road may have become in the meantime. Paris the *mezzadro* has come to better terms with his landlord than in the old contracts, contracts which in fact survived the war and only lost their force in the wake of the mass abandonment of the land in the 1950s. He simply farms the terrain in his own fashion and gives away 40 per cent of the produce to his absentee Florentine (including the best selection of grapes!). Nonetheless he and Leda remain *mezzadri* of our times, living reminders of an unjust but vital tradition.

Every evening towards 4 p.m. his small three-wheel Api snarls onto the parking place above the olive groves. He is probably bringing hay for the colony of rabbits, which he must feed and clean each day, ready to be slaughtered for the market and butchers in town. Whenever he is looking slightly sheepish at the door of his *cantina* and the cat is peering in greedily, I know that a skinning has just taken place. He sells about six a month perhaps, and at four pound a head, it cannot really be worth the continuous dutiful work. But it *is* work and I cannot see Paris sitting in a deckchair. Nor on a beach.

Recently in the hot summer days, when he appears more often at the *podere* to cut the vines with his thin, ancient, perfectly-kept scythe, or to water the tomatoes, make bonfires and collect fruit, he has taken to making an excursion with Leda, perhaps as far as the sea. But I have the feeling he regards it as a duty, a gesture to 'leisure' times. Anyway he is back soon enough and there has never been any talk of proper holidays. He and Leda prefer to go to the farm of their brother, which is on the plain and which he cultivates alone except when Paris goes to offer help. There they make 'holidays' by working on the grain harvest, collecting, pruning, digging the water drainage, and then eating together in the fields or with some other visiting labourers. As in the old days of *Feste campestre,* country festivals. In this way, Paris and Leda, who despite her job and a married daughter in an office, is of pure peasant stock, cling tenaciously to old traditions, to their blood. No matter that recently Paris has been able to afford his first new car, or that both of them occasionally appear in 'weekend' casual clothes, they are still determined to spend a good twenty hours on the weekend harvesting olives in a freezing wind or sweating up the hill with baskets of grapes on their backs. Without a word of complaint.

    Their own antagonism is reserved for the *padrone,* and in this they are traditional. They believe fiercely in work, its rewards and moral training, its surprises and occasions for showing tenacity, its contribution to their sense of survival in continually changing times. They are fully *mezzadri* even if they spend half their time in other jobs - jobs not geared to the earth but to the more abstract realms of money and the cost of living. Their *padrone* on the other hand shows a miserable indifference to work, at least in their eyes. He is a weekender who fiddles with plants, potters with the inside of the house, leaves wood lying around under everyone's feet, is concerned only with patios and mixing a little cement. To Paris this is little more than laughable. 'He begins so many jobs, but is he able to finish one?' he says. 'Send him back to Florence where he belongs.'

    Quite apart from the strong local pride this expresses, Paris' antagonism also comes from a deeper source. *He* works and produces. The other either does nothing important or interferes amateurishly with what is already done. One day the *padrone,* a youngish man with a moustache and an excess of arrogance, decided to water the new fruit trees he had planted (and, incidentally, horrified Paris' expert eye by splaying the branches and tying them in the shape of a crucifixion). He took the hose from his cellar tap and left it sprinkling the fruit trees all day. The result was a house and a farm without water, since the water system is a natural one and flows downhill, making its own water table. Fortunately, however, Paris reserved his venom for work in the fields. It was only then as we were scything grass on bordering fields that he expressed it. 'Doesn't lift a finger except to cause trouble. Go quickly, get some of the beans and he'll take the lot. You'll see. Next year I'll come and plant the tomatoes in your patch over there. At least you have water now. The thing with him is, the less he sees the better.'

This is the other side of his antagonism. If on the one hand he is hurt by indifference to vital concerns of farming like the drainage and water systems - water is as gold to any cultivator - on the other hand he will not prejudice his interest or those of his friends by confronting the *padrone* head on. His reaction to all such pressures, as the experience of centuries suggests, is guerilla action. If the *padrone* removes a hosepipe, tie it to a stake rammed in the earth. If he takes too much produce, take most of it before he arrives. But never let him see your *doppiezza* (cunning) too clearly. In his presence, retain the obsequious but doubting air of a polite servant, in his absence the true independence and astuteness of someone estimating and carrying out their own interests. How many times has Paris mentioned these words 'In your interests' or again 'We don't need to work here you know. We can leave tomorrow,' muttered when he has heard some particularly asinine comment from his *padrone* to us, his allies. It is a declaration of autonomy, even within the subordinate relationship. And it is carried out with the mobility of the guerrilla allied to the astuteness of the diplomat.

There are visual aspects of Paris which contribute to the impression of *guerriero,* or a buccaneer. One is the childrens' cowboy belt which he uses as holster for his faithful matchet. This matchet is used to quickly clear the inner growth of olive trees before beginning the pruning or to slice and clean the bamboo staves, which he collects in perfect formations for vine supports or as a sharpener of acacia stumps, which serve as parts of pergolas. Sometimes one can see Paris standing high up on the inside of an olive tree, aiming his matchet or stretching upwards at some high branch, with the tree sailing madly and exhilaratingly in the wind like any boat. Indeed before I knew anything about olive trees I was astounded by his tiger-like climbing and command as if a tree were really the ropes of a masted schooner. His face too is lined and tanned like an adventurer, with the flat nose and high forehead, starchy black hair of the typical Tuscan peasant. Yet he won't speak out of season. Sometimes a comment from one tree to another, a pause for rest and a chat while pruning the vines, an observation on the weather which he predicts perfectly, but in general he is taciturn, treating words as something to be spared for use at the right moment. Words are also energy, and in the fields he needs energy to support the ladder, carry sacks on his back, cut grass for the rabbits or strip trees of their olives. His way with the scythe is all stubbornness and concentration. He must clear between the vines on his *padrone's* land about four times a year. So he goes out and cuts all day, literally, with tense little motions looking from a long way off like the jabs of a sewing machine. At evening he will return with grass on his back and a narrow scythe slung over his back like a mediaeval weapon, ready for a little chat, watching everything on his way up the path. For that is another part of his personality – the eagle eye for changes.

He not only notices the weather, the approaching clouds or a fair patch. He sees every little change in a tree, or a water channel. He knows where the best grass is hidden, the best pears, a tortoise shell, a vine leaning dangerously, an olive uprooted. Every change of this sort seems to please him, for it means that the danger he expected is in fact on its way or has arrived. Life is full of approaching risks and one must be on the lookout, he seems to say. A harvest could be completely ruined. Indeed, if there is a serious change, like a big earth-slip or a wall down, a poplar across a row of vines, an animal loose in the cellar at night, then his fatalistic sense is fully flattered. He comes alive and starts to chatter as if he had just seen a wonderful play, as he has, in his imagination. For nature to him is a kind of play, a dangerous one, which we are here to predict and use if possible. This is the meaning of survival, the reason for country traditions and folklore, the challenge of being alive. It also connects him, or so I suspect, to a sense of childhood and youth. Nature is beauty, but it is fear too. He is fast at killing harmless grass snakes as he is ready to pronounce on the aesthetic value of olive trees. All over Tuscany one sees the aesthetic sense of the *mezzadro,* an alliance of traditional skills, the desperate need for produce, with the love of colour and beauty. Paris will pot flowers as well as kill snakes. The two go together.

As does a very strong sense of generosity with an acute estimation of his own interest, his own precise shares of the harvest. He will accept money for a certain things like a fresh rabbit but only on the basis of the price in town, which he follows exactly. But in general he tries to avoid money as the basis of exchange and prefers to offer reciprocal help, expertise, produce which he has but other's haven't. Everything thereby becomes a fluid system of unpaid exchange: land for tomatoes, which Leda then preserves and offers back in part, transport to the olive press or from the vineyards on our tractor in exchange for a large bag of walnuts. A rabbit each year for the grass he cuts on our land. And he is anxious to keep this exchanges going, not to rely on money, which is impersonal and ultimately unproductive of further contracts: a demi-john for wine, a sack of bruised apples for his brother's pigs, the remains of the *vinello* for making *grappa*. This reciprocal help is the expression too of the solidarity against the changing outside world, against the *padroni* and the exploiters, against the entrepreneurs who give less for a litre of olive oil than five years ago. There is no longer a possibility that a *mezzadro* can make a full living for his family without recourse to other employment or hiring himself out to agribusiness, there is no just reward for the amount of work involved, and even less in times of common markets and monopolies, but this system of exchange continues to function in defiance: the last redoubt perhaps against the pressure of indifferent capital, the obsolescence of peasant ingenuity.

'Tie it to the tree. You want the olives don't you? Just tie it at the top. Go careful.' So says Paris when I try to get up an olive tree at an absurdly steep angle to the house. Don't give up but improvise, is what he means. And that is exactly his approach. In the midst of his extreme stubbornness is this capacity for ingenuity as shown by that cowboy holster. In this he reveals himself as much a craftsman as a peasant. Indeed the craftsman is his closest ally – like Gistri the carpenter who lives at the bottom of the hill and makes the most perfect ladders and wine vats and benches. When Paris' wine vat started to leak in the period before the *vendemmia*, i.e. when the vat is filled with water, he banged at the wood for two days, again and again. His *padrone* thought him a fool. Finally, he filled the gaps with candle wax. It was ready – and he didn't have to pay for a new one. Other social classes, shopkeepers for example, tend to think him or Gino as a little below them. But with the builder, the craftsman, the carpenter and the wood-feller, they are at home. All need skill, and all need will power. The way Paris once forced our tractor to start was like a man pushing a mule, but he nearly succeeded. Now the tractor, of which he was at first suspicious, has proved it has the same will power as him: that will power which is needed to collect a hundred kilos of olives on a weekend or to feed forty rabbits every evening! Yet he would be the first to say there are more intelligent people in the world. 'Who knows where this tree illness comes from? After all, these things are known by more clever people than us,' he sometimes remarks. The difference is that he doesn't think this knowledge, which he respects, is enough to account for the many unknown factors of our life. This unknown belongs to an area of magic or at least superstition to which only the most experienced can get close.

When Paris sees something wrong in the way I am using a scythe or perhaps cutting a vine, he helps out with advice or a little example, but insists that this is not to *teach* me, for teaching would be presumptuous and a school matter which has little bearing on nature. The advice come rather from folk memory, the corpus of experience that may be imperfect but is the only guide we have at such moments. That and magic: the moon, the stars, chance and intuition, destiny. 'These things can happen,' he says. So too say the almanacs or *lunarii* which still circulate and which contain information on the moon's phases, eclipses, a guide for hunters, clear predictions of the weather, news of markets and fairs, advice on monthly cultivation (herbs for example should be planted on the day of the full moon). Ironically, these almanacs were first instituted by enlightened landlords to wean the *mezzadro* away from the habit of meeting up with others each evening in his *podere,* meetings called *La Veglia,* which were a kind of tribute to the oral folk memory, consisting of ironic poems on the subject of *padroni*, anecdotes and jokes, songs, excerpts from folk plays, readings from epic tales, most of which entertainment has now been replaced by the TV.

However Paris and Leda, like Livia and Gino, still invite one to visit at the hour of *La Veglia* (after work) and still relish gossip about bad landlords, good workers, exploitation by the government or the misery of the times, all expressed in the most colourful use of local examples and dialect. Just as the mountain songs are the freshest form of folk expression, so too is the declaration of necessary autonomy at its most intense in those places farthest from the city. A strong moral code too. When Leda speaks of her *padrone*, she asks 'What can you expect from a man without education?' But again the education she means is not the school sort or anything to do with knowledge in books. It is the way he has been brought up without realizing the difference between right and wrong, between good and bad. In the long run *mezzadri* often forgive the weak, they find extenuations, but they also insist that there is no way forward without a clear sense of good and bad, however clever you are. This for them is education, and they find it as lacking in the city suburbs they so rarely visit as in the TV programmes they are served. Paris and Leda by no means fully adopt the culture of the class to which they are 'subordinate'. They do not recognize 'leisure' or permissiveness, and their relations to the culture of this world are as ambiguous as their relations to the church and to their *padrone.* This is remarkable in a tradition which has seen so many upheavals and justified reforms in the past thirty years. One wonders if the generation of Paris is not the last to bear such strong witness to the quality of survival, so many gave up the battle and left the land in the 1950s and 1960s. This house was once a real *casa colonica* with three branches of the same family of farmers working and living here. Now it is divided into a part for amateur farmers, a part for foreign visitors, a part for an absentee landlord with a non-resident *mezzadro.* The story seems to be coming to its end.

However, when one sees Paris – or any other farmer in the neigbourhood – clearing out yet another olive grove, which cannot be possibly be producing until five years hence, or cutting back his trees stubbornly each New Year onwards, or arranging water for a new garden, planting nut trees, putting in new vines, it is hard to think that the process will ever stop. Work is the essence, and almost every work is geared to the future, to future subsistence or at least an imitation of subsistence. I know that Paris' daughter and son-in-law profit from his produce, but they do not lift a finger to help him. As far as they are concerned he is an anachronism. Their view of the world is not one of scarcity, nor one of protecting a patrimony of skill and experience against extinction, nor even one of admiring the strange ways of nature, its dangerous unpredictability. They do not know that we are all equals before this willfulness, that there is always a danger of scarcity and we must help each other in the just division of produce, through work and mutual aid. The television does not tell them that, nor any of their other sources of information. They are content that their eccentric father seems happy with his work and that they get a little out of it too: the rabbits, the preserves, the mushrooms, the nuts, the grapes and olive oil. They could of course buy them.

Paris' contentment seems to come from another source. In the same way he straddles an olive tree in a gale, he still has one foot in the world he understands. He refers with great glee to cutting grass on our land, calling it a *furto* (theft), and this recurrent joke is a reference to the *furto campestre* (country theft) at the heart of peasant folk-lore, something to be guarded against, indeed something which can still happen. One day we witnessed just such a theft of apples by two old women with sacks. Gently we took back the apples and then offered them some fallen ones for their animals. It was a simple enough event. But it gave Paris a whole fund of stories. It meant that his world, the world of scarcity, work, equality, justice, still existed!

Perhaps it was this which made him start singing, as he rarely does, that Sunday morning as he busied himself in his cellar, In a guttural voice he sang a folk song, one of those pungent tales of first love which the local choirs sing. And the way he was singing it was just as if he were saying: 'Look at me, the world is still intact and it's a Sunday morning. I've been working since sun-up and things are going well. No alabaster to carry today, no *padrone,* not even Leda. Just look at me.'

And soon I heard him at work again, sharpening his scythe.

4. The Olive Press

It is the day before Christmas. The next year will be momentous one feels. This year is nearly gone – and the olives are almost collected. They lie now in a cool inside room of the hut, once a pig stall, and on the floor of the big cellar, like a mosaic of green, blue, black little stones, a magic carpet, hand-woven. They have not been easy to pick this year. For one thing, the quantity is exceptional: the trees have only been rescued from abandon in the last five years but the worst are already showing signs of producing. Then the weather has tormented the late pickers with high winds and days of leaking rain. *Beati loro* ('Blessed are those') who started early, in the crisp days of November, for despite tradition and experience, nature ripened the olives quickly this year, even on these steep inland slopes away from the salt sea mist.

How the olive tree defines this landscape. All along the Maremma marshes and up the river valleys of Tuscany, across the slopes of the Appenines and over the Arno plain to the passes of Monte San Savino, the olive tree holds sway. Patterned on the beige soil in geometric perfection, rustling green and grey against the bright sea winds, sometimes silhouetted like a Japanese print against the sunset. Last night the whole spur of *Le Balze* merged black into the delicate outline of olives, cypress and ruined convent. Aesthetically perfect. The finesse of a master artist.

But it is not only a beautiful tree, cut as it is here in Tuscany into the shape of a wine glass with the molding of branches as on a potter's wheel. It is also of the greatest value to a smallholder, and in large quantities dictates the cultivation patterns of big farmers and agribusiness. Despite the net reduction in the price offered by the market on a litre of olive oil, even oil of the first pressing, the peasant and smallholder and remaining share-croppers still treat the olives as gold. He who is without olive trees is indeed a poor man.

If the harvest is a good one, like this year, some of our share-cropper friends go to pick olives on big estates. Gino and his sons for example. They receive a part of the oil they have picked, usually about fifty per cent when the process is completed.

On the kitchen wall of Gino's home is a calendar, which fills up towards Christmas with the amount of kilos he or his sons have picked each day. It is usually well over a hundred. His pride over this amount is controlled but visible, contagious too. A basket fills very slowly unless one is picking on the fullest of trees, and every kilo counts. One becomes avaricious as with gold, even picking olives by hand from the ground or from the nets which can be used on flat ground while someone beats the olives with a long stick. Here on the hills, the picking is mostly done with baskets slung from the shoulder and ready at the hip. It is a slower process than the stick and the net but also less wasteful. The garlands, should you have a good tree with garlands, go straight into the basket with a downward slide of the hand, rather than in all directions with an over-enthusiastic use of the stick. Besides, the trees have been pruned in this zone with the intention of making that swirl of downward-hanging garlands accessible to the hand, even if one is balanced on a wooden ladder. Only the uppermost branch, which is often left by the pruner in exclamation against the sky at the top of the main branches, only this one should be difficult to reach, but then can be cut at harvest time if full of olives. This is the system in middle Italy; Tuscany, Umbria, the southern slopes of the Appennines, the Maremma. In Liguria however, and Corsica, the trees – of a different quality – are left to bush like any plant and are always beaten with sticks. In Puglia and Calabria they are fashioned like huge antique sculptures, as old as Methuselahs, and drip down dramatically from their uppermost beam, gnarled and magnificent, but without that topmost exclamation which is left on their younger Tuscan cousins.

It is Christmas Eve and still it rains, a cotton wool mist and the wooden ladders have been taken in to dry. 'He who wishes ill to his ladder, wishes ill to himself,' a neighbour reminded me one day. He is right of course. The last ladder, an old one, had been left out often and one day cracked with me on it, split nicely in half. But I landed safely. The olive tree is a helpful partner for climbers and pruners. It offers three or four main supports and a network of cross footholds. It is also flexible without being an easy 'cracker', even in a high wind. Paris tends to prune the laden branches in a wind and to pick them on the ground but I rather enjoy the feeling of swaying up there as on a boat. Time has brought confidence with it, and pruning has eased the stretching to get those garlands into your hands. Only once have I come off fully, and that was a neglected tree which split in two, breaking me and the ladder's fall by its delayed action.

I am not alone in my enjoyment of this work. Despite having to clap the hands together against the cold, the olive harvest makes the fields alive towards Christmas with distant, high-flying conversations, jokes and songs. The more easily bored also play the radio, while they secretly compete with each other in the speed and quantity of their picking. As dark begins to fall, those cold, slightly flesh stones in your hand come thick and fast to your grasp, and you still can tidy the tree up by pruning here and there with your scissors or hand saw, taking a last rewarding branch or two to the house to be picked. With the hand saw, scissors, basket, belt and ladder, you are a true craftsman, and the laden cellar floor is proof of your passion. As you stare at it with the continued contemplation of standing in your tree, you mentally start to divide up its two-inch high surface into little bottles, sacks, jars which are salted away, glass or terracotta demi-johns, just as a butcher divides a cow. The eyes gleam with future possession, like the olives themselves in the moonlight of autumn.

Some local farmers sell their surplus, especially that earned in piecework, to cooperatives and agribusiness. Many, however, jealously store the oil in terracotta jars (the best) or glass demi-johns, selling a part here and there, but mostly saving the oil against the family's needs. An average family can consume up to forty or fifty litres of olive oil a year – and of course will accept no substitute. Ninety per cent of the oil produced in Italy is consumed here, but due to cheaper versions coming from North Africa or substitutes within the Common Market, the farmer receives less per litre for his produce than ever before. In a spare year he may just make a little money, but the proportion of work to profit is not an incentive for restoring abandoned olive groves or keeping the younger generation on the land. Practically no farmer works full time on his land. Even the brothers across the valley, who proudly keep their olive groves ploughed all year round, on the steepest of inclines, producing that magnificent terracotta earth beneath the blue-green trees, work half-day in the town. On Sunday they work all day in the fields.

Yet still there is a pride, almost an obsession, in evidence. After collecting comes to an end early in the New Year, Paris and his neighbours will bring the ladders back out to the groves and continue to cut back the trees, taking out the inside growth of little stems, shaping the garlands, removing wild branches. They may even tackle the black groves where trees have been left to grow over and the *fumaggine* has settled. The *fumaggine* comes from an insect which settles on sickly trees, hatching larva which in turn produce a black sticky dust on the leaves and branches. If this spreads, whole ingrown trees can become just a strangled black skeleton. A whole grove of these is a horror to see. They sometimes occur near dusty main roads, or simply in abandoned areas. If the disease is caught in time, a tree can be saved by radical but careful pruning, 'down to its underclothes' one might say. A year or two of consequent pruning, particularly where the little beard of growth begins again, can see an olive tree back on the way to health and production. Paris used to amaze me with his stubborn pruning of sick trees, he is a share-cropper who has no contract to care for all five hundred trees at the same time, but then I came to understand his passion - one which takes in almost every tree over a cycle of years. It is exactly the same sense of satisfaction I have known, looking back up the hill towards the house where my grove has also been pruned in time. Light falls glittering through the trees from a January sky as blue as the sea. It changes as it falls, the leaves reversing green and grey, the sodden grass below reflecting dancing shadows, new vines below that. All in its own liberated air and primary light. These trees will bring olives in two or three years, as they have done in times long past. If I were a better farmer I would dig round each one, as they used to do, and give them manure brought from far and wide.

But now it is Christmas Eve. We have to wait for those triumphing days, for the nervousness too which accompanies the delivery of olives in their sacks to the co-operative press. Paris will be nervous. Gino will be nervous. Mistakes must be avoided at all costs, in the sharing out, in the delivery. A terracotta jar of olive oil in the cellar is the focal point of the year's drama, more than the *vendemmia,* more than a visit from the *padrone* or the tax man. Before the season's chorus has stopped whispering the moment is with us again, returning cyclical upon itself. Like the ghost of Christmas past it is there in the olive branches winking with their half-hidden fruit, the little red hats of the aloes, the single white rose blooming on the wall of the hut. Returning, returning to the same point. A full cellar. No point in complaining of the weather. 'We are in December,' says Gino with the sing-song of his wisdom. Towards evening I go up to look out over the dark olives towards the dank, earth-smelling landscape. It cushions itself on the way down to the sea, billowing and sliding into blackness, marked occasionally by the distant flares of a car moving like a slow silkworm on a pile of straw. There is the shimmer of a Pisan suburb far away and a lonely farmhouse light on the hill. 'All is possible,' it seems to proclaim. 'The olives are safely in.'

Perhaps the olives of that house are among those which have filled the olive press to over-flowing in the holiday period between Christmas and New Year. Instead of the expected snow, which has fallen abundantly elsewhere in Italy, this region seems to have been singled out for occasional heavy rain followed by skies brimming with clear liquid blue and warmth – ideal for completing the harvest. There is nothing more discouraging than a damp or icy tree, nothing more sensual than picking up olives which are losing their stone-like coldness while a winter sun beats on the head and flashes in the eyes. After such days, if the eyes are closed, the inner eyelid remains stamped with the black olives against a green and blue background.

We have booked a place at the Olive Press, a co-operative of local workers and farmers. The foreman's hands are shaking with the effort of several weeks' abundance, but he is ready for us with a knowing smile. Men are men at the olive press (unless they are *padroni,* in which case they are amusing and rather over-dressed objects to be deferred to), for there is hard work behind those sacks. What is less recognized is that it is often women who have done it – certainly the major part of collecting off the ground.

At the house the atmosphere is nervous, intense. It seems that the whole ground floor is covered with this black-green carpet, a good finger deep, and wooden square shovels – or more recently, plastic dust pans from the grocer – have to be used to pour the olives carefully into sacks, cement bags, plastic refuse bags. Everyone is excited. Paris is here at the same moment to fill his sacks and bring his trucks down ready to load. The twilight, usually silent with no other noise than the rush of a distant stream, is alive with the scraping of shovels on flagstones. Finally the load is ready, the weight of eight *quintali* of olives distributed evenly between many sacks, since an over-full sack can be too heavy even to lift to a truck. We set off slowly.

Entering the Olive Press is like entering a very clammy theatre. The stage is set with a huge pair of grinding stones revolving in one corner, two centrifugal pistons pushing slowly upwards on what looks like a series of crushed door mats, pipes leading from sunken tiled baths, filled with a murky substance, to a steel tank system of filters and refiners, from which pours the thin stream of *olio extra vergine* (first pressing, highly refined). A set designed by the Vorticists: in which the workers with caps on their heads sweat and smile and watch the new arrivals with a certain canny interest.

First the sacks are weighed, one after the other. This must be done precisely, so that the co-operative's fee for each *quintali* (100 kilos) is properly estimated. It all goes down with a shaky hand into the foreman's book. Then a long discussion follows on the timetable of the process and the filling of the various containers, glass demi-johns, even terracotta vases we have brought with us. Paris is the leading figure in the discussion, which takes place at *basso voce* and with long intervals in between statements. The matter is agreed and hands are unfolded from chests. Work begins.

'They put yours on one piston, mine on the other,' explains Paris, pleased that things are to be done with a formal division. These men hate any confusion, any sign of the *dilettante*.

We wait on, for we are the audience as well as the participants, while the sacks are emptied into the vast grinder. Here the olives are mulched into an interesting mess of stone and paste which is eventually spread onto circular mats by means of a push-button funnel, like a cake icer. Indeed the final impression of the mulch spread round the mat is rather that of a baked strawberry flan. Everyone makes jokes about this, for the men are here to be entertained. There is not much else to do for the next few months, except prune the trees. But another conversation emerges almost at a tangent to the joking: work and life in the country.

It begins because Gino has entered with his *padrone* from Milan, a man in a camel coat, who is genial but has obviously never been in the press before. He seems the type who enjoys bar conversations and the little glass of wine offered him by the foreman covers any insecurity his irony encourages.

'But what do you do in the country?' he asks. 'Do you have frenetic entertainments in the evenings?'

Gino is arguing with the foreman – both have caps back on their heads – but Paris answers: 'City life is uncomfortable, all the tensions and the nerves. When I go in the country I just, I don't know, I just feel better.'

'That's because you have something to do.'

'Oh, the work is a way to pass the time well. We have nothing to do in town.'

'You may have a point. In Milan there is so much to do, I never know where to start.'

He is hedging and Gino knows it, now that he has resolved his discussion with the foreman, but he thinks it better to tip the wink: a sign of solidarity amidst the peasants, retaining their sense of humour. The grinders whirr on, mashing and mashing town ironies as the jokes begin to flow again. And the walls too, which are partly tiled. They sweat with the process held in by the cellar roof and bare earth. For the earth is hardened mud around the sunken tiles and in one dark corner are piled mounds of the remains of that mulch, once it has been pressed twice or three times (*olio di sansa*). These remains can be used in bricks for burning, similar to peat. And like any marsh land the air hangs heavy with the perfume of rich earth, human sweat and wine, the mulch of a year's flowering and twenty years', a hundred years' cutting, pruning, care. All for that thin stream of clouded green oil which pours unsteadily from the Vorticist machine.

'Do you know what my *padrone* did the other day?' asks Paris to pass the time. 'He took a ladder into the wind, left it there to fall over, and snipped at an olive I have pruned for twelve years. All the new side pieces I left to make the tree whole again, he cut off. He is a *maestro,* don't you think? He knows everything better.'

'And nothing at all,' adds Gino. As if the story were eloquent enough by itself.

The refining process is reaching its climax. Paris, wearing his blue overalls, which are exactly the same are those worn by the other men in the press, goes over to help lift, pour and shovel his olives from each of twenty or so sacks into the deep stone deposit, from where they are sucked in a large tube into the great grinders (a mad Roman chariot turning around itself). From there the mulch passes into a seething tank, like a bubbling volcanic blister, before being spread onto the strawberry flan mats and slotted onto the centrifugal holds. After he has finished his work – which is taken as normal by the others, there being no difference between one man in the fields and one man working the press – Paris goes to drink a little glass of red wine which he has brought along in a bottle like so many others. The bottles are clustered under the sink, a ritual gift from the farmers to the workers and sure evidence that the end of the process, this consolidation of so much work, is worth celebrating.

Finally, the cylinder with its mats is inserted into the dripping press and the relief shows on Paris' face. Even if the outcome was sure, there is still an element of uncertainty in his view of the world. Anything can happen. Indeed, just to prolong the feeling of suspense, he goes with one of the workers, a Harpo Marx figure with a *Toscanello* cigar constantly in his mouth, to inspect the refiner, from the side of which there exits a dark liquid like Guinness mixed with cold coffee. In order to check that no oil could possibly be contained in this mixture they take a clean glass and fill it, then let fall two tiny drops of the pure olive oil onto the dark foamy surface. The drops remain as they are, neither joining nor sinking – which is sure proof that the refiner's 1600 revs. per minute are doing their job.

Suddenly, for all the men present it seems that they have witnessed one of the few certain moments of their lives, lives spent in other jobs during the year. It's as if those terracotta jars were a visible security, one fear vanquished: whatever the falling price.

Later in the day, when all our containers are filled and placed in the cellars like prizes, Paris says '*Almeno l'olio è al sicuro*'. Forty per cent of it he must give to his landlord, but for a change there is no doubt in his mind.

'At least he olive oil is safe!'

Part 2: Panorama

5. The 'Stones' of Matera

In a country where the towns and even the cities are choked with cars, where every family member is proud to drive any kind of vehicle, and to avoid walking at any cost, it is easy to forget that the trains are just as full as the streets. In this long, fragmented peninsula, Italians are constantly on the move, and a train makes sense to the business man from the South, the student, the family visiting, the factory worker, the emigrant returning to his base.

The train is the home of that often-repeated comment, *pazienza.* The army, schools, farms and factories, offices, marriages and funerals, all are in some way governed by trains, by the resigned wait at the platform or in between stations. And nowhere is this resignation, this *pazienza* of delayed parting and arrival, the continual mobility and up-wrenching of roots, so visible as on the station platforms of the South. The land of emigration.

This morning I stand on the platform of Bari, waiting for the local train to Altamura and Matera. Such soft names caressing impatience with suggestions of an Arabic fort, high white walls and romance, dark eyes. But around me stand nervous men in their best, check jackets, their shoes gleaming, smoking cigarettes as their women-folk wait on big cardboard boxes held by string. After loading their men and the plastic containers of wine onto the train for the North, the women will return to their cars. Many of these have German number plates, having been brought down from there, and the station has big timetables for Milan, Switzerland and Germany. However, no one is going anywhere for the moment: a strike of one hour is announced on the station speakers and everyone sits down.

The only thing to do is to learn *pazienza* by taking a stroll along the promenade with its old-fashioned lamps and Mussolini hotels converted into apartments, towards the old town centred on its Cathedral. Life is revolving, people constantly on the move, zig-zagging, moving at a tangent, always moving through the streets. Near the Cathedral, in a real Southern *borgata,* the families live at street level with only a simple curtain across the door to hide the neighbours' view of children asleep on the bed, children playing, a television, a sideboard crammed with all kinds of mementoes and valuables. The neighbours criss-cross from each other's low house, or speak from different levels of upper windows as in a Goldoni stage set. Poverty is on display but also a certain affluence, a satisfaction of the spirit at least. There are shops for groceries or every kind of rope or local wine. There is a little knick-knacks market and good fruit to be bought, especially the medlar fruit. And always a sense of life flowing into life: unaggressively, naturally, modestly.

The Cathedral is almost blocked off by a football match that uses the sacred wall as a goal, while inside Verdi's death march is being practiced on the organ. I seek for a solemn thought but it is not necessary. Death belongs as much as the football match to this interval we call life, and as if to emphasise it an old lady in black mutters resignedly at both me and the boys as I cross the yard towards San Nicolo. There, the episcopal seat is held up by the most un-solemn grotesque one could imagine.

Returning refreshed along the main street, I feel relieved that I am a man here. Its status covers even a stranger with a certain no-nonsense respect, especially if he appears to be of modest means. Men of my sort are *ragazzi*, boys, workers, students or soldiers at some time in their lives. Many *ragazzi* travel, often alone, often to earn money in foreign places. They must be allowed to belong, and indeed there is a readiness, in the Southern mentality above all, to treat a man as a man – no more no less – as long as he stays within the correct limits and asks the right questions. He should be fed, cheaply and well, and he should think of women as vehicles for breeding, domestic work, or simply as sex objects. The cinemas next to the Cathedral are displaying pornography of the Nazi variety, I notice on my walk along the incredibly clean streets. These streets do not exist in the usual image of the South nor do the frequent public baths, which remind more of coal mining districts in Wales or Belgium.

My *pazienza* has been rewarded. The train to the interior stands ready on its single track. Autumn sunshine irradiates the late morning, fitting image to that expectant land within me I have called the South, Matera to its warm, old golden sound. Eccentric too. I have to sit in a broken armchair like a dozen others, unhinged from the floor, within a carriage which is more like an elegant hotel saloon fallen on hard times. The train shunts off with its load of grizzled labourers and office workers, through the industrial suburbs of Bari, and gains speed. Soon the cement gives way to deep-rooted cultivation and I sink into an almost horizontal position in my armchair, parallel to the ancient olives which in endless groves bend down their upper claws to create a gnarled skirt lower and even more abundant than their younger relatives in Tuscany. In the middle of them are stone shelters, round as a hermit's dwelling (some are inhabited), with feathers of cactus growing, isolated in sea of vines. Walnut trees come next, their thinner branches cut as finely as the olives themselves, and everywhere the colours of nature are turning gold, brown, the terracotta red of many vine leaves. As if to mark the extraordinary human care visible over a vast number of acres.

It cannot last for ever. Before we reach Altamura we are all squeezed into a single railway wagon and as we proceed the cultivation gives way to wasteland and bare hills, fallen stone walls. Poor Altamura! Like so many hilltop towns of the South, it is nothing more than a lost conglomeration of ugly apartment blocks built mainly with Mussolini's money, or on a cheap speculative basis since the war. Needless to say, the anti-seismic laws were not respected.

However, the real surprise follows as low sunlight from the sea picks out white huts dotted on ploughed fields, fields which seemingly reflect clouds, but which are in reality scudded by the soil colours themselves – a re-enactment of Nature's turning leaves – beige, cream, reddish, chestnut. A landscape in continual illusionistic movement, almost like the people themselves, high up on the 'heel' of Italy.

The little train reaches Matera of the soft, dark name. This time it does not disappoint. Indeed, after that landscape how could it? The students, soldiers, priests and mothers who emerge from the train into a waiting bus have the same chestnut looks of that name, a dark untouched beauty residing in the eyes, the amber skin, the black hair. And this beauty is reflected in a mixture of shyness and interest. They want and do not want to say hello. On the bus which takes us into the town where the youngsters crowd around the terminus, a boy sitting opposite smiles again and again at me without speaking, without breaking that spell of communication. As he leaves the bus he picks up his horn from the floor and later I see him enter the conservatory of music. But he could just as well have been one of the teenagers sitting on their motor-cycles in the main square. All show a similar need to know something new, precisely because they haven't been given things on a plate, because they do not *know* already.

In a nearby bar, where the owner in cardigan and glasses greets the clients as if he were their favourite uncle, I overhear a conversation between a young man in his early thirties and a grizzled, red-face farmer. The youngster defends the methods of his new co-operative farm, saying that it took thirty years for his stupid father to discover irrigation for the fruit trees. Now they have a system of watering by proper technical means. Why were the elders so stubborn? Because they're afraid of the risks, he says. They fear it's the end.

I leave and walk on down the main street. Matera has its fair share of the newish apartment blocks but this main street is still lined with splendid seventeenth century houses and palaces. A handsome street of chemists and council chambers. Then suddenly the street gives onto the *Sassi,* the 'Stones' of Matera; a cascade of old, partly antique houses built into the rock on which Matera stands and now almost entirely empty of inhabitants. In the last fifteen years they had moved out to those blocks. I take a winding stairway downwards to the prickly shade.

The small houses with their square windows and doors now stand open and deserted, mirror of an Etruscan settlement or Capitoline Rome, the black squares of their masonry like a gaping valediction to a lost communal culture almost empty of echo. Where once there were those families in continual movement as in the *borgata* of Bari, relatives and neighbours hailing each other from different storeys, donkeys to transport hay and wood, the first Vespas for the ambitious, now there are just a few old men and unemployed youngsters tidying up as in a cemetery. A smelly, damp valley of social life gone, almost all gone. The end of the beginning, as our governors would remark. Thank goodness! Meanwhile the clambering monuments stare out myopically onto the caves of the opposite hill, the locked-up sepulchres and Mount of Olives landscape deserted by all but the cars in the tourist car park. Will it be an arts and crafts market in the future? A national beauty spot? There seems little to be done.

For the reason has gone for its survival, as simply and effortlessly as that. In the last fifteen years a mode of existence which outlasted centuries has disappeared, leaving practically no sign.

Sadly I walk back up the empty roads where one or two youngsters have squatted in the graffitied ruins, towards the Cathedral. It is hard to get there. The square is full of cars and photographers waiting. Inside however there is some comfort, a suggestion that not all links with the past have been broken. The Cathedral shimmers with cheap gilded effects, with candles and Madonnas and a radiant silvery altar. Before it stands the priest and his bridal couple while suited guests and their children wander in and out of the back door, seeking relief or fresh air or simply a quick stroll. There are flowers everywhere, a sugar-candiness which will soon be repeated at the marriage feast. But for the moment the organ laboriously plays Gounod's *Ave Maria* and an old man's voice, gulping and tearful, swelling like a sail in a storm and then sinking into nothing, chews Gounod's phrases into a microphone. The church bell is being pulled in rhythm. A moment of pure sentimental drama. This land is still the home of Verdi, if less of the communal life he knew. *Pazienza.*

Travellers are to need it back at the terminus, waiting for the bus, and then again waiting at the Altamura for the connection south. I sit in the station park for my picnic of fizzy local wine and *mozzarella*, happy to be a moment in the shade, even if the sun is autumnal. Suddenly a blaze of horns surrounds the square of pines and the wedding party deposits the two newly-weds on the green sward for their pictures to be taken. I can only wonder what is so romantic about the station park at Altamura. Is it really the only green available in this area of rich, soft landscape? No, but it does have some modern sculptures of a nondescript variety, humps of white stone, and beside these the young couple form and re-form in romantic, noble, faithful poses, before stepping back gingerly over the pine needles and into their car. Next week these photos will be proudly on show, among many others, in a window on the main street of Matera. And in the couple's new home.

Not as it would have been once, a small house near relatives in the '*Sassi*', but a third-storey mini-apartment in one of those shaky white blocks on the edge of the town.

6. A Funeral in Crotone

Crotone. If Italy were to stand on the balls of its feet, there would be Crotone, a modest, forgotten town, left much to its own devices in a wild hinterland. Nonetheless the approach to it along the side of the Gulf of Taranto reveals some surprises. By the yellow sands and the calm sea rear up at continuous intervals unfinished developments. Some are even inhabited as they stand, but most are just left open to the elements on three or four storeys.

What are they doing there? a traveller might ask. I was told that they represent a man's investment for the future, even though the speculation, which is often illegal, cannot be completed at the moment (a restaurant, apartments-by-the-sea). These nightmarish girders sticking from cement are waiting to be bought or simply to appreciate in value. This they do, even if unfinished, because the land is by the sea and the sea means potential profit for August. They have been funded by money from the Cassa del Mezzogriorno, a fund which favours this kind of local speculation (and has much to answer for in the earthquake zone), or by the savings of returning emigrant workers who see in this an investment as well as a material marking of their return to the locality. This expression of their status, as well as of their sacrifices for their family, has been learnt in the countries of their work. One is not allowed to forget that this is a land of emigrants, communities decimated by the economic pressures of emigration and by the faltering will to survive of those who remained. In the aftermath of the great Calabrian floods of thirty years previously, it was precisely on these 'developing' coasts that the transplanted shepherds and peasants of the interior lost all identity and connection with their tradition. At least the ruins of Pompeii speak of a past experienced. These sad new ruins speak only of a dead present.

Crotone stands amongst its olive groves and a no-man's land of terminals and apartment blocks. By the sea there is a curving promenade along which gather hundreds, or perhaps thousands of youngsters in the evening, festive and noisy, eating ices and watching, watching for fun, for a flirtation, for an odd character to laugh at. They jump and kick at each other like playful animals, snuggling against the emptiness of the hinterland, warming bright faces in the tangled, garish light of kiosks and bars and bumper car stands. They wander down onto the shabby, but pleasantly normal beach, improvising their entertainment between swimming and Coca-Cola, football and Vespas. While behind them rear up ornate apartment blocks, following on round the shape of the bay to the scraggy, red-sanded hills on the edge of the town. The hotels are friendly and empty. Sellers of contraband cigarettes walk up and down past their entrances. *Grazie* and *prego* are to be heard continually on the air, as if politeness here had a real function, was a part of that huddling together and the wider solitude which is expressed in social convention. It makes the wheels of contact move more easily. A thriving, directionless town, with its fair share of suburbs but also with a shopping centre amidst the older buildings and churches.

A vivacious shopping centre, defiantly alive. It is thronged with people as the sun lays its magenta along the deep main street, outlining the luxurious palms, competing with the flashing pink *Euromoda* sign of a large store. And everywhere this enormous bustle and throng, the movement and noise of laughter, car horns, children demanding, grows more intense as the clock moves towards eight o'clock and the end of the *corso* hours. Finally the lovers cuddling amidst the scant secrecy of the town park and the noise of a boat unloading are told to leave. The shop doors close and the great evening roar subsides just a little.

The next morning the same process repeats itself, but for a very different reason. It is eleven o'clock. I have just visited the market with its vast range of copper pots, porcelain, fish and vegetables and fruit of all sorts. A seething market of peppers and tomatoes and a thousand varieties of olive in great bulging sacks. It is then that I hear it.

The sound is that unmistakable, immensely melancholy one of a town band, slightly out of step and tune, running through their repertoire of funeral marches. But as the same time there is a warmth about those sliding brass cadences which is immediately and appealingly Southern. I first heard it on the island of Ischia, a band appearing from round a corner in order to serenade the patron saint while a wooded rock in the sea underwent its yearly burning. And it has the same effect as then, a tightening of the heart's muscles, softness and nobility, quite unlike the more martial laments of the North.

There in the midst of all those shoppers and the glaring light of the morning comes the huge funeral procession. A local dignitary of some sort, or his wife, carried on the shoulders of male mourners who are all dressed in their normal everyday clothes. There is no fuss but a constant flow of movement, a dignity in movement, as the team of coffin bearers exchange the heavy coffin without halting for a moment. An effect of sliding along everybody's shoulders. A completely natural accompaniment to the rhythm of the music and the unhurried, unceasing steps of the large procession of mourners. The death belongs to us, as much as we to it, and indeed as the coffin passes the shop fronts are pulled down and both the shoppers and the assistants come out on the street to pay their respects. No one hurries off. The traffic ceases and each one, even the youngsters and children, pay unaffected tribute to death as it passes.

I wonder if this is the virtue of Catholicism, this easy integration of death in life, this familiarity with the life beyond. There seems for a moment to be no clear break between our being surrounded by the saints and joining them in the everlasting. But then, as I glance at the young and not so young faces around me, I realize it is not only a matter of life being passed in the antechamber to paradise. For these people, born and bred in the town as many of them are, have yet remained close to the earth. It surrounds their little town and its shabby port. It is their hinterland, and a spiritual hinterland too. Our there beyond the olive groves and stretching upwards towards the mountains of *La Sila* lie the fields and the little hamlets from whence came their ancestors. And the break of continuity, the break of relationship between them and their forebears has not been enough to destroy that very resistant peasant tradition to which, for all their shopping sophistication and modern apartments, they still belong. I have just come from the market. It is quite unlike any I have seen in the North of Italy. The sellers and farmers and buyers belong to each other in a bond impossible to locate but clearly there.

And the way the coffin is carried through the streets of Crotone under its communal witnesses, the witnesses of an entire community, is the expression of this as yet unbroken bond. Life is an interval, says the peasant tradition. We return to our forebears in the cycle of time. Our will to survive and our awareness of mortality, these are the things we have always experienced and they cannot be hidden, neither from children (the other part of the process), nor by the benefits of progress or technology. This interval needs no overblown celebration, no pompous priests, no artificial aids, no embarrassment. We belong to each other in death as in life. And it is this which seals the communal bond of where we came from, whether we are now shoppers or office workers or small business-men. The uniform does not matter, only the fluency and simplicity with which we recognize our dead. The children and grandchildren for whom they have made their sacrifice belong to the future. It is the dead who return to the past, and so to themselves.

For a few minutes we continue to contemplate that which belongs to us. And then just as easily, the coffin surges up to the Cathedral door, the band reaches the end of its repertoire, and the traffic moves on again. There is a moment for everything in Crotone.

7. In Search of Verga

> *This story is the sincere and dispassionate study of how there must probably grow and develop in the most humble conditions the first itchings for affluence; and what kind of disturbance must result in a family which has lived relatively happily until then, the vague longing for the unknown, the realization that one is not well off, or that one could be better off.*

So wrote Giovanni Verga in the preface if his edition of *I Malavoglia*. Published in Milan in 1881, it is the story of a Sicilian fisher family, living in the heart of the ancient community of Aci Trezza, which slowly breaks up under the pressure of new economic and social demands. Their life of simplicity and proverbial wisdom and codes of exchange or honour is drowned in the waves of progress as irretrievably as their boat, the *Provvidenza*, sinks in a storm off the coast of Sicily along with their eldest son. It was this story which inspired Visconti to make the film *La Terra Trema*. It was the social witness and breadth of Verga's vision which inspired D.H. Lawrence to translate the fables of Sicilian peasant life collected in *Novelle Rusticane* ('Little Tales of Sicily') and also *Mastro Don Gesualdo,* the story of a man higher on the social scale, a bourgeois in a provincial town, but again destroyed by his avidity for riches.

Now, a hundred years from the publication of *I Malavoglia*, I have come to Sicily to seek out Verga's settings, if such still exist: the beach of Aci Trezza, the two jagged rocks hurled by the giant Cyclops after the fleeing Odysseus, the comfortable bourgeois background of his childhood in Catania (where he was born in 1840 and died in 1922), the flat malarial plain of Lentini which is the scene for the *Novelle Rusticane*. That social process which he first described in the 1880s, the extinction of the peasant tradition, is reaching its end. I wonder if this journey will tell me something of how long there is to go, or what – if anything – will be salvaged.

The train from Messina follows on down the magnificently rocky coast, passing spare little hamlets, painted boats drawn up on the beach, smallholdings with tomatoes and beans, Taormina elegant and corrupt on its high promontory, miles of magical lemon groves. There is a sense of life, mystery, every acre used, much more so than on the Calabrian coast. The old houses are inhabited instead of being abandoned in preference for empty futuristic structures. In the interior one can see toy-town villages perched on rocks, mountains and poor pastures. Etna appears, smoking magenta in the sunset, and in front of it the town of Giarrè with its faceless apartment blocks surrounded by cultivation. Even from the train one senses the intensity of those lemon groves, the rather intimidating, aching beauty all around, the elegant old villas of nineteenth century Gothic mixed with Byzantine.

Aci Trezza, however, is the scene of the first disappointment. The station master (of the same station where Ntomi waves goodbye to his mother and his girl from the military train which will take him away to his death) does not think much of Verga hunters. He refuses point blank to accept any luggage in deposit. It is a warm, milky day. The sea is over a mile away. I try to outflank him with logic.

'But they have been taken everywhere else in Italy, on the station.'

'They must have a lock,' he replies. He wears a red flat hat and sports a scrubby grey moustache, the liquid sad eyes of the Sicilian.

'But there is nothing of value in them. They are not lockable.'

'They must have a lock.'

'But the railway has taken them everywhere on the mainland.'

'Then they were wrong.' His eyes flare briefly and he turns on his heel. There is nothing for it but to walk with two overnight bags. Comparison with the mainland was perhaps not such a good tactic. Sicily is not in fact Italy, although men of his type admire the relative discipline of its army. We do not look very disciplined.

But as we trudge downwards towards the bay, I see another reason for his attitude towards foreigners – and foreign ways. Aci Trezza has become a zone for holiday developments. The process which Verga first described has reached its apogee here in the villas and hacienda-style villages which clutter the low skyline, the Alfa Romeos with Roman or Neapolitan number plates. Yet, despite being surrounded by the monied twentieth century, the old disappointments still seem to linger on. The little port itself, where the *Provvidenza* was several times patched up and where La Longa scanned the tempestuous sea for the return of her husband, is now a kind of marina with motor-boats and wind-surfers. The Cyclops rocks have remained of course, a continuing warning, and there are signs of ancient Trezza in the ship-builders on the wharf where red trawlers are being constructed all of wood, in the nets still being picked by young men and boys alongside their boats with the single-coloured stripe, in the row of old houses which clamber down to the shore where the washhouse once rang with the gossip of the good wives about the Malavoglia and what they would do to save themselves. One can see from this little nucleus of memory how exceptionally beautiful it must have been, even to Visconti's eyes in the 1940s; though now no one tends the remaining olive groves and the people in general are hostile, cynical, with that shallow worldliness which tourism and television breeds.

We turned back to Aci Reale, where the Malavoglia once went to sell their goods at the market each Saturday. It is a handsome town more sure of its communal self than its sister by the sea. There is a splendid seventeenth-century square with fine baroque churches and a palace. The streets bustle like Crotone with life and shopping. Everyone, form the age of twelve onwards, seems to have a motor vehicle and uses it endlessly for the sheer pleasure of it. The stink and roar is continuous. But the greatest activity is in the market, especially the fish market. Here men still shout their goods, displaying huge sides of tuna fish as big as an elephant's leg, sharks and other creatures of the deep. In such a place the sea becomes what is rightly is – another primordial world, one with which we can have only the most fragile and dangerous relationship, so mysterious and unknown is the element, so living with beings who mock our dry impotence, our cackling and calling and immobility. Our lack of poetry. In the market of Aci Reale the fascination of the Malavoglia for that other world, the drama it contained, is at last almost tangible.

The next stop is Catania, where Verga studied law at the University and wrote his first novel *Amore e Patria*. It is riddled with plaques commemorating his birthplace, residences, visits. His family was well-off, liberal-inclined, of aristocratic origin, and that is the first impression of old Catania: avenues of eighteenth century buildings with ample proportions and wide streets, the Via dei Crocifissi with its almost Jacobean decorations, the University, the long gracious main avenue down to the port with its expensive shops and evidently high standard of living on show. Catania of the suburbs is rather different, a stage-set for shoot-outs between rival gangs of the underworld, those who control Catanian business and politics. But here in the centre it shows a face much less dilapidated and problematic, much less choked with poverty and cars than Naples or Salerno. The well-off entertain themselves with classical music in the decorated cake of Teatro Bellini, elegant and historicist in its classical quotations, spacious, remembering the part it once played in Italian cultural life (no longer, from the evidence of the concert we heard), and incidentally in the work of Verga. The less obviously well-off attend a meeting of the Communist Party in the square nearby, addressed with splendid controlled rhetoric by the Presidentess of the Lower House. She is enlisting the patriotism of all Italians in the fight against political corruption and regional indifference. I remember that Verga once founded a political magazine with patriotic intent called *Rome of the Italians*. He would have enjoyed the meeting.

> *And you feel you could touch it with your hands – as if it smoked up from the fat earth, there, everywhere, round about the mountains that shut it in, from Agnone to Mount Etna capped with snow – stagnating in the plain like the sultry heat of June. There the red-shot sun rises and sets, and the livid moon, and the Pleiades which seem to float through a sea of exhalations, and the birds and the white marguerites of Spring, and the burnt-up summer: and there the wild ducks in long black files fly through the autumn clouds, and the river gleams, as if it were of metal, between the wide, lonely banks . . .*

Verga's malaria as described here fortunately does not penetrate the train from Catania to Enna, but a sense of the arid plain does – vast and empty and dry it reveals itself before the train turns to the north with Enna following in its wake. It is a countryside of lemons on the upper slopes, and dark brown, reddish ploughed fields, the occasional oasis of vines or olives. An emigrant, just back from Frankfurt after forty-five hours on the train, points it out with the resignation of someone who gave it all up a long time ago:

'Here there is too much work,' he says, amused by our enjoyment of the views.

'Too much for little reward?' I reply.

He doesn't answer immediately but indicates a brand new villa-type house which somehow has been built in this agricultural wilderness. 'It costs a lot of money.'

He grins, and I grin back. At Paterno we pass a goods yard of some sort with a few steam trains in their sidings. He scratches his head. "Here we have old trains. In the North they have new trains, but they would pay a lot of money to buy old trains. How can you win?'

Enna approaches on its hill like in a John Ford western, Indian country. But in fact the castle on its hills is Norman and the church Arab. Alongside us glint still blue lakes and the snaking vital motorway, empty of traffic.

The Sicilian continues to talk. He seems to like me, despite my accent, or perhaps the many hours of travel make him sympathise with me as a stranger. He has bought a piece of land near Agrigento and is going to build on it for the wife and children he has left there. He seems amused by his job in Frankfurt. When he started many years ago, he shoveled fibre into threshers twelve hours a day. Now he has a button and a seat! 'And before there was too little money for too much work. Now they pay me too much for doing nothing.' Yet he is still admires Germany and the firm. 'It has discipline,' he confides.

The track snakes its way through some of the most beautiful country imaginable, especially as the setting sun picks out and clarifies the contours, the fantastic mountain shapes. The land, mostly planted with wheat, varies from rust to beige to light green. There are well-kept very precise vineyards in the French style, a few inhabitants, huts of brushwood like wigwams in the fields, donkeys passing, cacti distorted in the near-view, ancient broad olives toward Monte Calogero on the left. It is April but the wheat is already half collected. So ordered and careful is the approach of the farmers here. A pastoral landscape with rare flocks of sheep and yellowing, volcanic contours.

My search for Verga is coming to its end. Soon we will reach the coast and then the oil refineries and those empty cement structures towards Messina. The Sicilian wants to tell me a final story.

'When I was young I went to France with three friends. We didn't speak a word of any French, but we had been offered work at a farm near Lyons. When we arrived at the station it was snowing. No one was there to meet us. But one of us had a piece of paper with the farmer's name on it. We phoned him and he came. At first he was puzzled because he didn't expect four workers, but eventually he took us on all together and he billeted us in the outhouses. Everyday we rose at 5 a.m. for the animals, with five *merenda* in between. One of us made very good pasta. We all liked the work but after two months the farmer had to send us away. The farm was being mechanised.'

8. A Neopolitan *Sceneggiata*

Everything is theatre in this doomed city, from the *zampognari* humping their bagpipes along the gallery on Via Roma to the vast receptions of the Communist mayor in the Palazzo Municipale, from the Spanish liveries of the *carabinieri* to the dark suits and gowns of the audience in the glittering San Carlo. Theatre is the stuff of life – of business too. Contraband cigarette sellers still operate on the steps and streets, in the sprawling market where a tourist is immediately recognised. Gypsies beg in the railway carriages, sit on pavements with their children, compete for attention with the prostitutes of the port. There are horrendous stories of gang murders, different factions of the Camorra shooting it out all the way down the coast to Salerno, for here there are protection rackets and monopolies over practically everything. Any glance at the skyline reveals the savage speculation which the city has endured in the last thirty years, and at the same time, its enormous housing problem.

The real Neapolitan proletariat and poor live in the *Bassi,* called ghettoes by the progressive urban architects and their backers. The numerous, convoluted back streets are the stage of the poor, the backdrop to an intensely communal life which thrives on an intangible system of exchange, black work, traffic in kind and child employment. In these clambering narrow streets, families live crammed together on the ground floor of their dwellings as if they were already out on the street, and children take turn with working parents and relations in the large communal bed. The community is all, and the strong passions of living and despair, of death and celebration, are played out on a public stage of neigbourhood. All under the eyes of the Madonna at the corner of the street, affixed to the wall of a house, shining in Christmas-tree mercy.

Language too is the stuff of this living theatre. The will to survive is expressed in a continuous and well-known game of *battute* which will render a stranger immediately visible, an alien presence. Theatre and language are the expression of this extraordinary people's determination not to be mown down by the hand of fate, the daily vicissitudes of Nature or the decrees of a condescending, distant government. Business, cheating, *battute*: Naples can only survive through its dialect. It is the natural home of Eduardo de Filippo, of pantomime, of folk theatre and dressing up. The Neapolitan expects from his theatre a ceaseless flow of himself, his daily actions and language, his victories and defeats. He has little time for heightened language and artistic relief. His life is already drama enough.

Sandro explains this to me. Sandro is of peasant stock and has studied hard to become a successful maker of films. He is still very loyal to his family who live near Benevento and are rightly proud to their son. Like many self-educated men, Sandro is a theoriser, a fluent theoriser who will leave few intellectual stones unturned. He smokes countless cigarettes, has the beard of an intellectual, the swarthy complexion and black eyes of generations of Spanish colonisers, but the stocky gait of a farmer. When he speaks high Italian Sandro is a little dull. In Neapolitan dialect he becomes vivid. All resides in the *battute* and the expression: as it does in the *sceneggiata* we are going to see.

We take the funicular train from the Vomero, the heights where the middle class live, down towards the Via Roma. Facing us in several tiers are long lines of Neapolitans sitting as if at school or in some strange, devilish play, while the wagon slides narrowly downwards. At the bottom, we walk through an area of the *Bassi*. A slice of moon hovers in the early autumn sky above the noise of TV sets and squabbles. A pile of rubbish and plastic burns with a dull flame that blackens the already blackened walls of a church. As usual the church is locked and surrounded with bars. It is practically impossible to visit churches in Naples.

Suddenly a lone child calls out something to us in a half-friendly voice. I clumsily reply and Sandro has to ward the child off with a stream of dialect, so that she will not start to beg. We reach the theatre safely.

It stands in a side street behind the railway station and is evidently one of the most popular and famous in Naples. The piece we are to see, *Monte Vergine,* is announced on bright posters outside with the picture of a boy on the back of a man ascending a long, long mountain path. The boy's face is one of pure suffering innocence.

We enter the theatre with difficulty. People good humouredly jostle each other to get to the ticket barrier where the feeling of excitement is encouraged by the policy of only letting in a few at a time. The start of the performance is still a half hour away, but no matter. A chance like this cannot be missed. Indeed my eyes are already brimming with the drama of the evening.

Once inside, Sandro indicates where we must sit to get the full impression. The full blast too. A band is warming up with some dance and folk tunes while the audience take their seats. There are many children present, whole families including grandma and grandpa, lonely ageing bachelors, shop girls and youths. The uproar of conversation and greeting is tremendous, even more so than in the streets choked with little cars and evening walkers. Ice cream cartons and *noccioline* packets litter the floors and the smoke of a million cigarettes floats on the air. Every so often children dash in and out of the toilets, which stand completely open to the hall.

Slow handclapping starts and whistling. Loud jokes on the air. There seems more anticipation for this play than for a football match between Naples and Milan. Suddenly the brand reels into a particularly loud *Tarantella* and the audience settles a little. The curtain rises.

A country scene with two facing houses is painted on the crude flats behind three microphones spaced across the stage. No nonsense about projecting here. We are in Pantomime Land, and indeed each new character that appears on the stage sings a song that is greeted with wild applause or, in the case of a villain, jeering and whistling. But at the same time there is a curious absence of burlesque or even the kind of slapstick which might help things along in other places. Here the story is related through its cardboard characters (the child, the priest, the father who emigrates to America, the wicked uncle who belongs to the Camorra, the wholesome mother, the jealous tart of an aunt) with total dependence on the emotions as expressed through the brilliance of the *battute* and the perfect timing of the moral clinch lines. These are awarded on a tennis-match basis to those who show the most honest and truthful feelings.

I am as captivated as my host. The technical simplicity, the watching of a drama played back to us who are somehow up there moving the flats ourselves, jeering and booing and applauding, clapping in time to the magnificent Napoletana musical interludes (vamped eighteenth century folk tunes), going wild when the victory of true emotion actually occurs, is didactic in effect but without the accompanying sense of distance. I notice an old man to my right whose face runs with tears when the Madonna effects the miracle of the boy's healed leg, a leg made lame in a fire caused by the wicked uncle. And this emotion allied to technical crudity goes even further when we are invited to watch a short 16 mm film of the cast ascending the *Monte Vergine* in person before the final triumphant, redemptive scene. But it is not only the old who are touched. The young cramming the front stalls seem to go mad, interrupting and commentating each twist of the morality.

There is a pride and innocence in their reactions that is far from the sophistication and knowingness of their northern cousins, far too from the disco glitter culture of those better off. This crude *sceneggiata* is theirs, belongs to them, reflects the communal experience and problems of their everyday drama. The priest of course, is shown as very randy and can only be cooled down by a linguistic joke at his expense. Poverty is shown as the breeding ground for gang warfare, where only honour can redeem. Sex is shown as needlessly repressed and yet subject to codes. True is opposed to false emotion, real love to possessiveness, forgiveness to violence. All in a language which is both humourous and touching, all orchestrated by the most vibrant singing of each member of the cast, who compete with each other in the strength and originality of their inventions. Naples and theatre, an approach to survival. Sandro tells me that a new piece – *O Trovatello* - is already in workshop for Christmas.

Meanwhile we are back on the streets, the theatrical streets of Naples, and are hungry. Sandro sees an apt way to conclude the evening. '*Facciamo un giro,*' he says, his black eyes sparkling like new coals.

A *giro* can mean anything from a visit to the tobacconist to taking the boat for Palermo, but I go along willingly as he drives the car through a series of the most complicated back streets, zig-zagging up and down one-way systems and impossible turn-offs until we reach a quiet road on what may or may not be the outskirts of the town. In fact the lit Madonna at the corner suggests that we are back in the *Bassi*.

Anyway Sandro has found it. Judging from the amount of cigarettes he smokes, he is in a rare mood, perhaps because like any normal Neapolitan he adores driving. The fluency, risks and sheer wild improvisation are all part of everyday fun (a fun that horrifies visitors).

We park the car haphazardly and cross the street. All the ground floors along the street are in fact a few steps down like cellars or dens, and it is one of these we enter. Inside there is a simple room like a village hall, some tables and chairs that vaguely suggest a bar, and a large fridge. Mirrors occupy one long wall, in which are reflected several bohemian faces. Apparently they are waiting for Sandro to appear. As greetings are exchanged, Guido comes from the back kitchen to welcome us with the usual *battute*, which I do not understand but which Sandro seems to settle to his advantage. Guido begins to conjure a meal from the scraps in the tiny kitchen – a few *lasagne* here, a pork chop there, salami and *peperonata,* wine from the bar round the corner. His only helper is an adolescent boy wearing an apron. It all seems both serious and comic. Guido is a portly severe man with no-nonsense eyes and a hatred of pomp and circumstance. However he is a soft as a young girl when it comes to discussing the menu – the tribe waiting are mainly Sandro's actors – and the state of the stomach, hence mood, hence ability to survive daily problems, of each individual.

Sandro again explains to me. These, he says and points at his loud actors, are not the regulars. Guido has accepted us for tonight, but usually he cooks only for the *transvestiti.*

The *transvestiti!* I glance up at the road lamps outside. The road is halfway up the door, another stage set where we await the real actors. Towards one o'clock in the morning, when we are all fed and drunk, they appear for us the audience-voyeurs. Exhausted, they clip-clop down the stairs from the car whose wheel rim can just be glimpsed from the door. They are astonishingly tall, perfectly made up and wigged, with feathers and extras, as shy and quiet as the audience is loud and too merry. They appear like so many fragile birds, nervous ostriches, and sit at a far table while Guido hovers over them like a worried aunt. Coca-Cola from the fridge, pasta and a little meat. They are dog tired.

While these working youths eat, removing for a while their wigs but not their make-up, Sandro explains to me their precise role. Again it is pure theatre, illusion for sad hearts. The *transvestiti* have no license for cars; they are not allowed to drive or to street-walk by the city police. They are therefore carried to various bridges of the city by their 'chauffeur' (also their pimp) and are picked up by lonely men, mostly married men who understand completely the illusion they are seeking. It is not normally a sexual liaison, for obvious technical difficulties, but a romantic one. The married man pays the transvestite her company, her bonhomie, her ability to flatter the man's image of his romantic self. They sometimes go to restaurants, to bars, or the cinema, occasionally to a dance. In this way the married man remains faithful to his wife and to his religion. His liaison is a harmless diversion, unproductive but vitally important to a marriage of boredom.

'In Naples we learn how to help each other,' says Sandro. I can only agree as I stare on at the group of feathers and rouged faces, reflected a hundred times in the mirrors of the room, the men-women with low delicate voices and their gazelle shyness, offering the rest of their Coca-Cola to the now stunned audience. Naples and theatre, a fantastic communal culture; one made up of make believe, of *battute* and survival. The art of survival as magic, I think.

But eventually it is Sandro who drives me home, in a Fiat not a pumpkin.

Epilogue
The Ruins Management

The commuter train for Pompeii passes through the strange no-man's land of little factories and fruit fields below Mount Vesuvius. This is Camorra country, where the hand of the ruling bosses lies on every enterprise and smallholding from here to Nocera to Salerno, a tight triangle of thuggery that mixes generous protection with clan warfare. We see little of it from the train window. Some tomatoes, canning factories, many vines. And then the long lines of filthy tenements towards the sea.

Yet the sea glitters in the bright sunshine, liquid gold further out, near at hand just a floating dump for garbage. Countless Neapolitan children swim and play amidst the rubbish, walking through smashed warehouses towards the grey-black beach. Some of the boys, faithful to their tradition for theatre, flash their pride at the train and shout as it passes. We however do not shout back. We are concentrating on Pompeii.

At the station there are the usual tourist stalls and guide books. These are repeated on the main street to the ruins and it is interesting to note how many are intended for Italian tourists as well as for the usual foreigners like us. Their presence is announced on the bus fronts in the square or outside the restaurants: Verona, Torino, Bologna, Bolzano. Their cars are also here in force. For it is the weekend, and affluent Italians count their heritage as a dutiful part of their weekend diversions in a way unthinkable even five years ago. Unfortunately, once inside the ruins one sees that the duty weighs heavily. Guide book resumés are read out as the bored visitors and their children quickly pass on to the next ruin. There is a kind of stubborn comprehensiveness in their approach, which makes them willing to tip the foxy guardian so that he will mechanically inform them on what is in fact quite visible before their eyes. Several times we heard 'This is a dog, this is a bird, this is a lion,' in places one could not enter *without* using a guardian. The disease is not exclusively Italian but here at Pompeii they seem rather expert at its transmission.

However, with a little selection and luck, the effect of Pompeii on ready eyes can be tremendous. Even with all the closures and the poor state of conservation, even with the evidently rapid decline towards extinction, the spirit soars at what has been recovered to us since the first tentative, dazzling discoveries.

It is not only a question of the size of the ruins, covering such a large area as they do. It is also the other physical aspects of this *villegiatura* suburb, which comes to us replete with all kinds of modern bourgeois characteristics and is yet 1,900 years old. The wheel tracks of the coaches and carts are still worn into the street stones. There are foot crossings from one house to another. There are wine shops and bakeries, most of all the conscious cultivation of art and elegance in these open, otherwise severe villas. Snobbery is rampant. A close look at the Vettii, Menandrus and Misteri villas is enough to show this. The dark reds, blacks and sometimes primrose backgrounds to the finely imitative decorations are an equivalent to William Morris interiors: and then on the walls are still lives, street scenes, little angels brushed by the wind, architectural games, dogs and birds, *putti,* gracious ladies and not so gracious grotesques, just as in any comfortable country house. Only the frankness towards sex strikes one as more modern than our present middle class might find acceptable, at least as part of the dining room decor. And indeed, obeying the prudery of earlier times as well as the salacious interest of some Ministers of Public Works, most of these startlingly frank pieces have been removed to a special room in Naples or are hidden from public view. However, an enterprising Southern hawker has come up with the idea of collecting them together under one cover and selling them in a special edition called *Forbidden Pompeii.* In this way prudery has made them as forbidden as the attitude of the youths at Torre Annunziata when the train passes. And their gestures just as obscene.

But Pompeii is still a shock, from the aesthetic inspiration it has given to painters as different as Ingres and Moreau to the mystery of its alignments in art: the flatness, the sculptural values, the non-perspective strange for eyes used to the Renaissance. And these painters were certainly not the masters of the time. Perhaps the Villa dei Misteri frecoes are the most disturbing – the human-size allegories and mysterious symbols which, without really looking AT you, nonetheless speak around you. In and out of the structure.

This melancholy grace impresses for a long time after the visit, and the feeling is something to do with the simple reminder, ominous as it was, that civilizations flourish only in a comparative sense and that they carry within them the seeds of their decline. Thereafter all that is left to admire is the strength of their mythology.

What I wondered, would be left after our 'deluge', what would a similar contemporary resort look like if it were depopulated? Clearly this *villegiatura* community had a strong connection with nature. Communal life and art flourished in these surroundings. Yet if such a disaster happened at St. Moritz a few *Playboy* magazines would be found, some luxury bathrooms, mysterious facial creams, ski boots and central heating pipes, electric hair curlers, mini-bars, showers and saunas. And if it happened along the Neapolitan or Calabrian coast? Later generations would discover moon cities of second homes and unfinished cement structures, 'cathedrals in the desert' as the Italians themselves call them. And in the meanwhile, what of the rural or communal cultures which still survive but are fast being engulfed by these symbols of our times, and all they represent?

As we leave Pompeii to return to Naples, I read a notice which I find, in its broken English and anguished tone, a melancholy comment on the moment. I cannot know that within a few weeks an earthquake will prove it to be chillingly apt.

THE PUBLIC IS ADVISED THAT RUNNING MAY CAUSE UNPLEASANT ACCIDENTS. THIS ANCIENT ENVIRONMENT IS UNCOMFORTABLE AND IN FACT RUINED, BEYOND ALL MEASURE OF SECURITY.

The Ruins Management

Available from Amazon in Paperback and Kindle editions

THE SCENT OF INDIA by Pier Paolo Pasolini
translated by David Clive Price

'Moment by moment, there is a smell, a colour, a sense which is India.' So wrote Pier Paolo Pasolini in this collection of essays describing his visit to India in 1961. Pasolini captures the shimmering, magical quality of India and also sharply records the terrible poverty surrounding its beauty.

Widely admired as a film director, Pasolini's talents as a novelist, poet and political essayist are rarely recognised outside Italy. This vision of his visit to India, translated by David Clive Price, provides a fascinating insight into India and into Pasolini's own obsessions and ideals.

'Pasolini's journey is chronicled with characteristically feeling perceptiveness.' Times Literary Supplement.

'*The Scent of India, beautifully translated by David Clive Price, has many moments of religion in everyday life that bind Pasolini in a spell that he tries to recast over his readers.*' Time Out London

ALPHABET CITY by David Clive Price

As his marriage disintegrates in a welter of suspicion and accusation, Peter begins to discover an identity of which he was previously unaware. He tries to escape his past and recreate his identity by fleeing to America. There he is drawn into the bleak sub-culture of lower Manhattan and at the same time into a devouring relationship with Joe, a black actor. The two of them leave on a dare-devil trip, running drugs through the south-western States, a trip that takes on the mysterious contours of pursuit and self-destruction...

'*David Clive Price has extracted the heart of New York and delivered it alive and throbbing on the page. This is the underworld that few tourists ever see. David Price has seen it with great clarity.*' Edmund White, novelist

CHINESE WALLS by David Clive Price

Set in the culturally and financially linked cities of Hong Kong and London, this novel couples a serious critique of contemporary business and social mores with an exciting whodunit and a secret love story. Full of the sights, sounds and smells of both cities, the novel explores the difficulty not only of relationships that have to meld both East and West, but also of family commitment and work, ambition and emotional fulfillment in the globalised world of today.

'Set in a world normally associated with high stakes, but not necessarily with intensely personal human dilemmas, this novel delivers page-turning drama even for those unfamiliar with the banking scene in both London and Hong Kong. One watches nervously as the narrator steps out onto the tightrope stretched between driving ambition and private and family loyalties, not knowing - as we do - that the safety net is being slowly dragged from under him. Highly recommended." Peter Moss, author of the 'Singing Tree'

'If you read his book, you will enjoy being appalled, titillated and at times excited, but don't expect that you will be reading just a work of fiction." Nigel Collet, Fridae.asia

MOONLIGHT OVER KOREA by David Clive Price

This journey into the heart of South Korea takes the reader from the birth of democracy and the hosting of the Olympics Games in 1988 to the brash, sophisticated, highly creative Korea of today. On the way, the writer pauses at Korean temples, mountain hermitages, the border with North Korea, romantic islands and ancient capitals to evoke a portrait of a country in constant, dynamic flux.

'David Clive Price has travelled widely throughout the Far East as a travel journalist and writer. He has a long association with South Korea, having written about the country for many international publications over a period of thirty years.' Periplus editions, Singapore.

Printed in Great Britain
by Amazon